OILS
AND THE ENVIRONMENT

IAN MERCER

Stargazer Books

Printed in U.A.E.

Editor: Katie Harker

Designer: Phil Kay

Illustrator: Louise Nevett

Picture Researcher:
Brian Hunter Smart

Library of Congress Cataloging-in-Publication Data

Mercer, Ian, 1944-
    Oils and the environment / by Ian Mercer.
        p. cm. – (Resources)
    Includes index.
    ISBN 1-932799-31-1 (alk. paper)
    1. Oil industries–Juvenile literature.
    2. Oil industries–Environmental aspects–
Juvenile literature. I. Title. II. Resources (North
Mankato, Minn.)

HD9490.A2M46 2004
333.8'232–dc22   2004041615

CONTENTS

OILS AROUND US

Oils play an important part in our lives. We depend on oils for cooking and cleaning, to make paints and plastics, and to run cars and ships. There are many different types of oil, but each belongs to one of three groups—mineral oil, animal oil, or vegetable oil.

We fry food in vegetable oil and lubricate engines with mineral oil. But all oils—whether they come from fish, sunflowers, or from rocks underground—are made from substances that are, or were once, parts of living things.

Mineral oil is drilled from rocks beneath the earth's surface.

Vegetable oils, animal oils, and mineral oils are widely produced around the world. Some of the world's largest crops—like corn, cotton, and soybeans—provide us with vegetable oils. We get animal oils from farm animals and fish. Mineral oil (or "petroleum," the Latin for "rock-oil") is extracted from the ground.

Peanuts are a good source of vegetable oil.

Fish are an important source of animal oil.

OILS FROM PLANTS AND ANIMALS

The most common vegetable oils come from seeds, nuts, and fruits such as sunflower seeds, peanuts, and olives. Animal oils come from layers of fat under the skin, or from organs like the liver. Many plants and animals are rich in oils and fats, which they use as a way of storing energy.

Fats help to build parts of the body, such as the brain, nerves, and the retina at the back of the eye. Eating a balanced diet, with some fat, helps to replace the oils and fats that our bodies use.

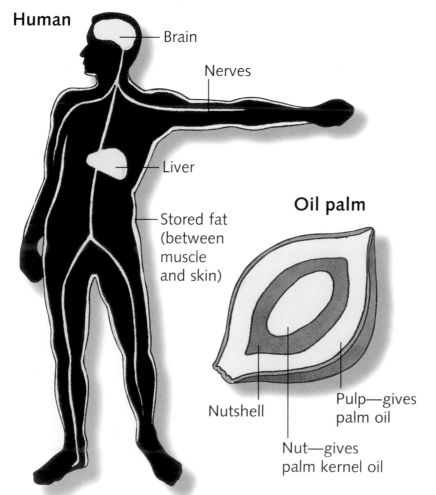

Human

Brain

Nerves

Liver

Stored fat (between muscle and skin)

Oil palm

Nutshell

Nut—gives palm kernel oil

Pulp—gives palm oil

Oils and fats in animals...
Oils and fats are foods that contain a lot of energy. Many animals, including humans, store fat under the skin. This fat provides good insulation against the cold. The brain and liver are both rich in fats.

...and plants
Plants fill their seeds, nuts, or fruits with oils and fats. The fruit of the oil palm, grown in the tropics, is picked for its oil. Palm oil comes from the outer flesh of the fruit, while palm kernel oil comes from the inner "nut."

A closeup image of human fat cells taken with an electron microscope

GROWING AND HARVESTING

Throughout the world, animals and crops are farmed for the oils and fats they contain. Animals such as cows and goats are bred for their milk, which is rich in fat. Some of the milk can be made into butter and cheese. Other useful oils come from sheep, pigs, and fish such as tuna.

Vegetable oil crops are grown in huge fields. In the United States, millions of acres of land are used for growing soybeans, sunflowers, and corn. After harvesting, the seeds or fruit are transported by ship, truck, or train to special mills where the oil is extracted.

Sheep are farmed for their wool, meat, and oils.

A sunflower field in France.

EXTRACTING OIL

Oil is taken from plants and animals using a process called "extraction." Oil mills are used to extract vegetable oils. The seeds or fruit are first cleaned and stored in huge containers called silos. Then the oils are extracted using pressure, heat, or chemicals. Sometimes two or three processes are used.

Animal oils are extracted by heating. When the fat is boiled or steam-cooked, the oil can be skimmed off. The fat from cattle, sheep, and goats is called "tallow." This is used to make soap and candles. "Lard"—used in cooking and as lubricants—comes from pig fat.

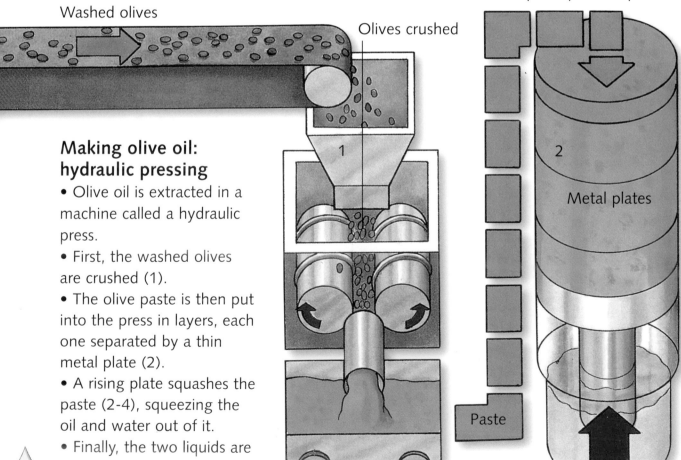

Washed olives

Olives crushed

Olive paste put into press

Metal plates

Paste

Making olive oil: hydraulic pressing
• Olive oil is extracted in a machine called a hydraulic press.
• First, the washed olives are crushed (1).
• The olive paste is then put into the press in layers, each one separated by a thin metal plate (2).
• A rising plate squashes the paste (2-4), squeezing the oil and water out of it.
• Finally, the two liquids are separated by spinning (5).

10

Olive picking in Algeria

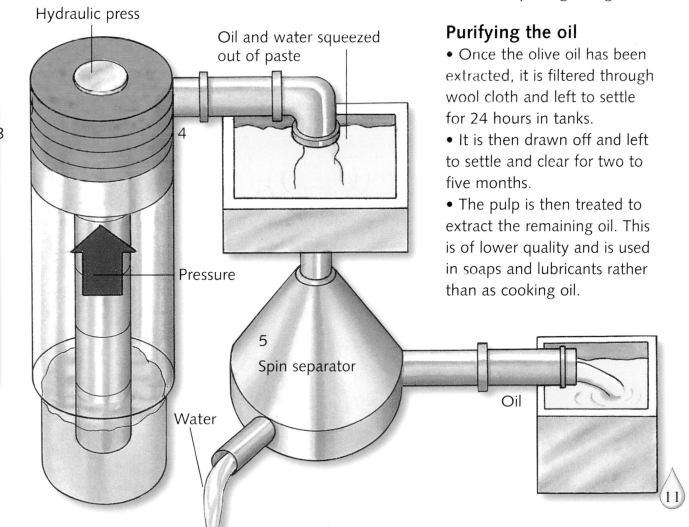

Hydraulic press

Oil and water squeezed out of paste

Pressure

Water

3

4

5
Spin separator

Oil

Purifying the oil

• Once the olive oil has been extracted, it is filtered through wool cloth and left to settle for 24 hours in tanks.

• It is then drawn off and left to settle and clear for two to five months.

• The pulp is then treated to extract the remaining oil. This is of lower quality and is used in soaps and lubricants rather than as cooking oil.

SOLVENT EXTRACTION

Applying pressure is a good way to remove oil from seeds and fruits, but it does not remove all the oil. To extract the remaining oil, a process called "solvent extraction" is used. When a solvent is poured over vegetable pulp, the oil dissolves. The oil can then be separated by heating.

Some oils, like soybean oil, can only be extracted by solvent extraction. The soybeans are rolled into flakes that are easily soaked by the solvent. Soybean is the United States' largest crop and the country produces large amounts of soybean oil.

Extracting soybean oil

• First, the soybeans are cracked open, lightly heated, and flaked. Then the beans are fed into a moving chain of baskets.

• As the chain moves around, a solvent made from petroleum is poured over the beans. This dissolves the bean oil. The process is repeated to dissolve as much oil as possible.

• The flakes are then tipped out and the solvent and oil mixture is piped to a distiller.

• The oil and solvent are separated in the distiller using steam heat. The oil is extracted and the evaporated solvent is condensed in a cooler, spun to remove any excess water, and reused to dissolve more oil from the baskets of flaked beans.

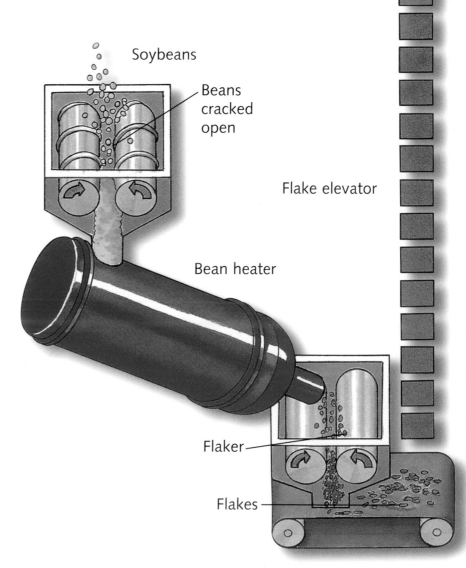

Soybeans

Beans cracked open

Flake elevator

Bean heater

Flaker

Flakes

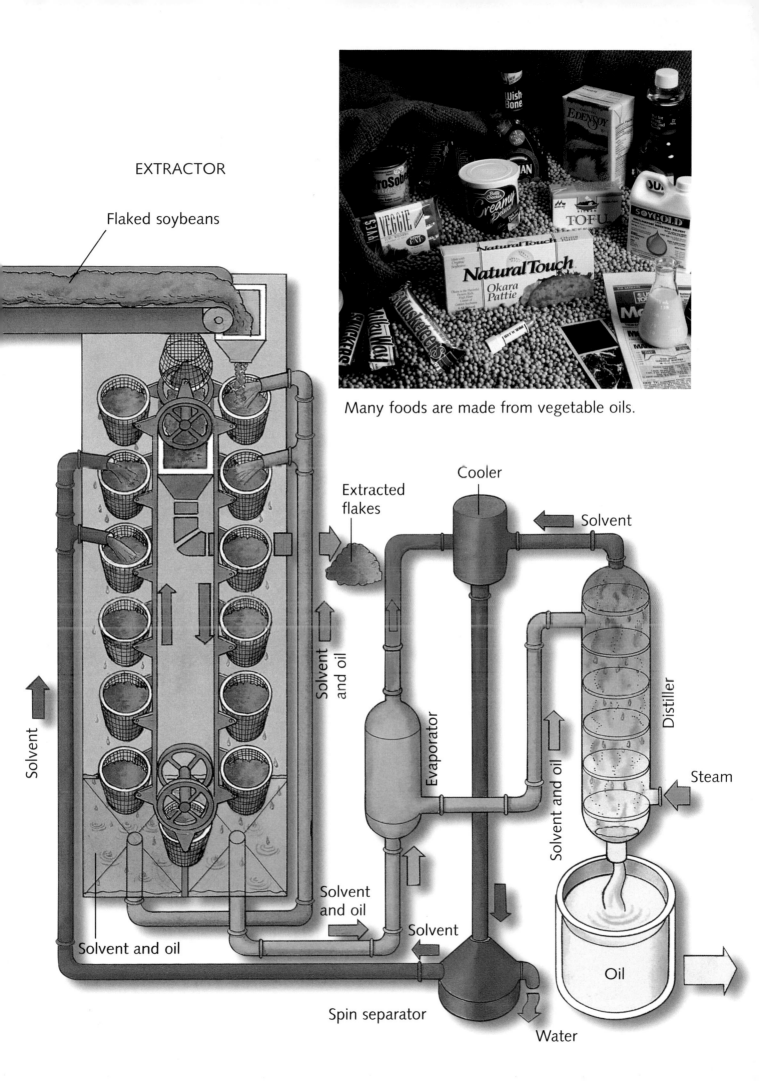

EXTRACTOR

Flaked soybeans

Many foods are made from vegetable oils.

Solvent

Solvent and oil

Solvent and oil

Extracted flakes

Solvent and oil

Cooler

Solvent

Evaporator

Distiller

Solvent and oil

Steam

Solvent and oil

Solvent

Spin separator

Oil

Water

HOW PETROLEUM IS FORMED

Unlike animal and vegetable oils, mineral oil (or "petroleum") takes millions of years to form. Petroleum comes from the remains of tiny water plants and animals. When these organisms die, they settle on the seabed and are slowly buried by mud and sand. Over millions of years, heat from the earth turns the oily parts of the organisms into petroleum.

Natural gas (mainly "methane") is often found with petroleum. Natural gas is widely used for cooking and heating. It can be refined to produce "liquified petroleum gas"—a useful domestic or vehicle fuel.

300 million years ago, the earth's climate was warmer and the ground was covered in bogs and swamps.

14   Mineral oil comes from the remains of animals that lived hundreds of millions of years ago.

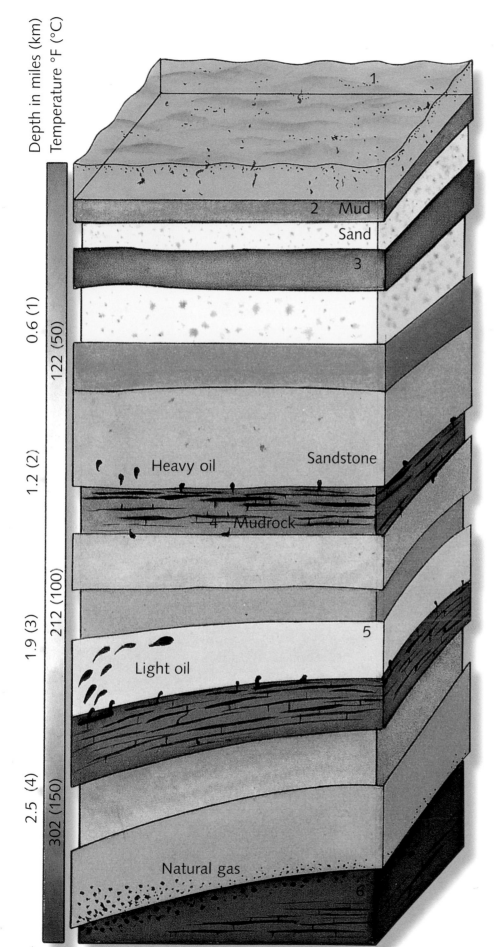

Depth in miles (km)
Temperature °F (°C)

0.6 (1)
122 (50)

1.2 (2)
212 (100)

1.9 (3)

2.5 (4)
302 (150)

1.

2 Mud

Sand

3

Heavy oil

Sandstone

4 Mudrock

Light oil

5

Natural gas

6

Oil and gas formation

1 Just beneath the surface of a lake or sea, tiny plants and animals (or "plankton") use sunlight energy to grow.

2 As the plankton dies, it settles on the seabed and decays in the stagnant mud. Some of its oily and waxy parts are preserved.

3 These change into dark brown specks in the hardened mud. The stored sunlight energy is buried deeper and deeper.

4 Where the mudrock is buried deeply, it becomes hot. The specks in the rock begin to ooze with thick, heavy oil.

5 The deeper the rock is buried, the hotter it becomes, and the more oil is produced. When the rock becomes scalding hot, it oozes with light, runny oil.

6 As the rock gets hotter still, the oil released becomes lighter and lighter. Eventually, natural gas (mostly "methane") is produced.

FINDING PETROLEUM

Mineral oil and natural gas are valuable resources and a lot of time and money is spent trying to find them. When oil and gas are formed, they rise upward through the rock. Some oil and gas escapes at the earth's surface, but some becomes trapped beneath a layer of leakproof rock. The oil and gas deposits (or "fields") are held in the pores of the rock, like water in a sponge.

Special techniques, such as "echo-sounding," are used to provide geological maps of underwater areas. These give a good indication of where oil and gas fields may exist. But the only way to be sure that oil is present is to drill a well.

Finding and extracting oil and gas

Geologists search for likely areas where oil and gas may be hidden beneath the earth's surface. They know the sort of rock formations that will trap oil and gas. Some traps are formed by dome-shaped rock layers (1). To find traps like these, sound waves are used in echo-sounding (2). The traps are then tested for oil or gas by drilling test wells—called wildcat wells—into them. To be worth extracting, there must be a large amount of oil that flows easily from the rock.

When oil or gas are discovered beneath the ocean, production platforms may be built (3). These carry power plants, factories, drilling rigs, and hotels for the workers. The oil and gas are extracted through wells at different angles. Water is often used to help force the oil out.

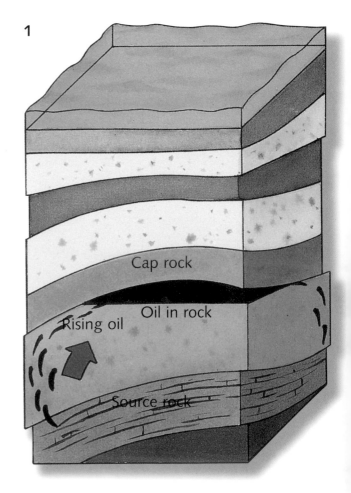

1

Cap rock

Oil in rock

Rising oil

Source rock

Oil can also be extracted using a mechanical pump like this "nodding donkey" pump.

2

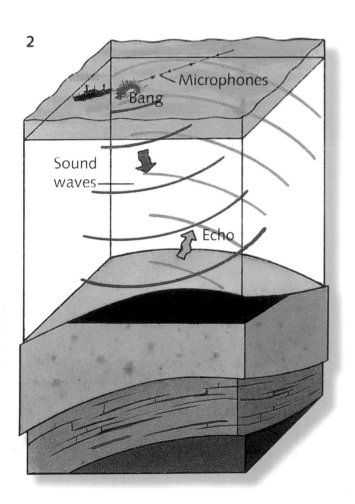

Microphones

Bang

Sound waves

Echo

3

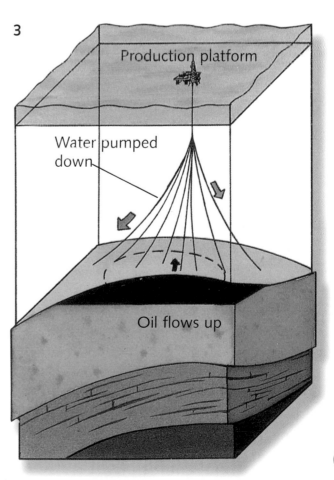

Production platform

Water pumped down

Oil flows up

17

OILS—A CLOSER LOOK

If we take a close look at the chemical structure of different oils, we can see that they all have something in common. Oils are made up of billions of tiny building blocks called atoms, that join together to form molecules. The molecules that make up oils all have a similar structure—they are made up of chains of carbon atoms with hydrogen atoms attached.

Mineral oil (petroleum)
• The molecules that make up mineral oil are called hydrocarbon molecules. They are built of hydrogen and carbon atoms.

• The carbon atoms join to make chains (right) and rings. Some chains are very long, but most are shorter than 20 carbon atoms. Natural gas has the shortest chains.

Animal/vegetable oils
• Animal and vegetable oils are made of carbon and hydrogen, but they also contain oxygen atoms as well.

• Each oil molecule is made of three carbon chains joined to a glycerine molecule.

• Glycerine molecules have carbon, hydrogen, and oxygen atoms arranged in an E-shape.

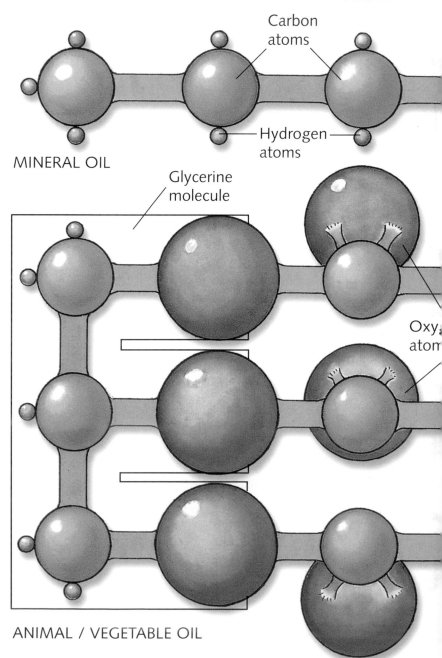

Carbon atoms

Hydrogen atoms

MINERAL OIL

Glycerine molecule

Oxygen atoms

ANIMAL / VEGETABLE OIL

18

Two fats that we eat all the time are butter and margarine. They are made of millions of tiny water droplets set solid in fat. Fats like these are solid because their carbon chains are strong. Other oils, made from short, weak chains are runny at room temperature.

Oils and fats feel greasy because their carbon chains slide past each other and make them slippery. Sweet-smelling plant oils called "essential oils" have a different atomic structure to greasy oils. They are "liquid" oils that have been distilled from the leaves, stems, or flowers of plants.

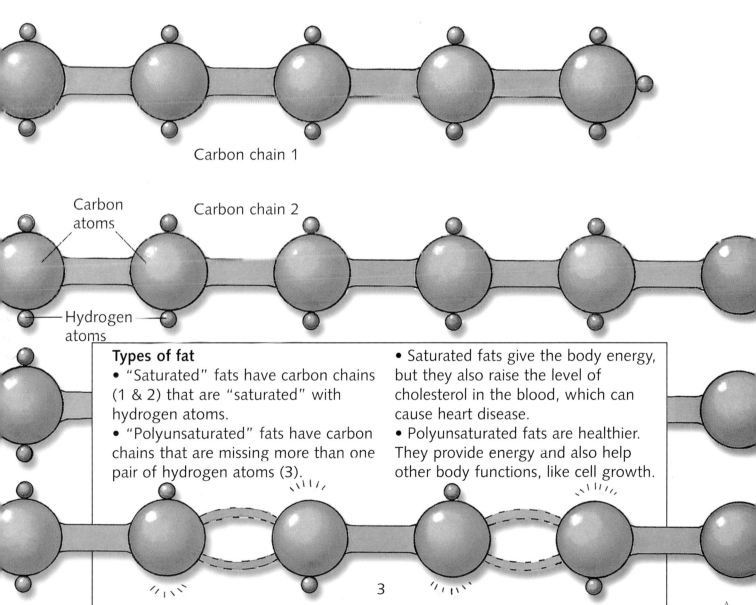

Carbon chain 1

Carbon atoms

Carbon chain 2

Hydrogen atoms

Types of fat
• "Saturated" fats have carbon chains (1 & 2) that are "saturated" with hydrogen atoms.
• "Polyunsaturated" fats have carbon chains that are missing more than one pair of hydrogen atoms (3).

• Saturated fats give the body energy, but they also raise the level of cholesterol in the blood, which can cause heart disease.
• Polyunsaturated fats are healthier. They provide energy and also help other body functions, like cell growth.

3

REFINING AND REMAKING

Most oils are filtered, purified, or processed before they are used. Animal and vegetable oils are treated with chemicals to lighten their color. Raw mineral oil (or "crude oil") is shipped or piped to an oil "refinery." There the oil is purified and separated into different products, such as petroleum gas, gasoline, diesel, and kerosene.

The carbon chains of many oils are altered, or remade, to produce more useful substances. For example, removing hydrogen from carbon chains creates weaker links. Oils with these weak links are more easily converted into products like plastics.

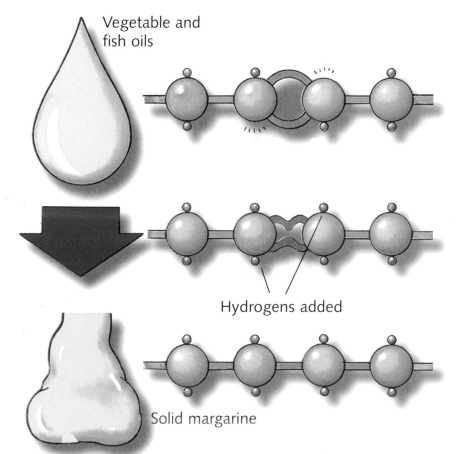

Vegetable and fish oils

Hydrogens added

Solid margarine

Adding hydrogen atoms

• Oils can be converted into other useful products by adding hydrogen atoms to their carbon chains.

• Margarine is made from vegetable oils and fish oils. Hydrogen is added to these weak, polyunsaturated carbon chains to harden the oil and produce fat.

• Hydrogen is added by mixing hydrogen gas with hot oil under pressure.

• Just enough hydrogen is added to make fat that is soft enough to spread easily. If too much hydrogen is added, a hard fat like tallow can be made.

Cracking

Gasoline is one of the most useful oils that can be extracted from crude oil. To get as much gasoline as possible, some of the heavier oils are separated again by splitting their long carbon chains. This process is known as "cracking."

Heat breaks carbon chains.

Smaller chains produced

Mineral oil is processed in a refinery.

OILS FOR THE HOME

All kinds of chemicals are made from oils and fats. If you look around you, many of the things that you see will be made from these chemicals.

When you are out shopping, look at the labels on food and drinks to see what is in them. Watch for all the different kinds of cooking oil. Most plastics are made from petroleum (mineral oil). How many different kinds of plastic can you find?

This page outlines some of the products that are made using oils and fats.

Mineral oils

• Mineral oil (petroleum) is used to make paint (left). But its most important use is as a fuel for vehicles like cars, trains, and airplanes.

• Grease and lubricants made from mineral oil keep machinery in our factories running.

• Petroleum can be processed to produce plastics. Many objects are made of plastic, including dishes, clothing, and even car bodies.

• Fertilizer can also be made from mineral oil.

Animal fats and oils

• Oils from animals such as whales and cows are used in some cosmetics, soaps, and candles (right).

• Most animal oils are used for food processing, cooking, and baking—as butter and lard.

• Most soap is about 75 percent tallow, which comes from the fat of cattle, sheep, and goats.

• Animal oils are also used to make printing ink, glues, vitamins, medicines, perfumes, detergents, sealants, and lubricants.

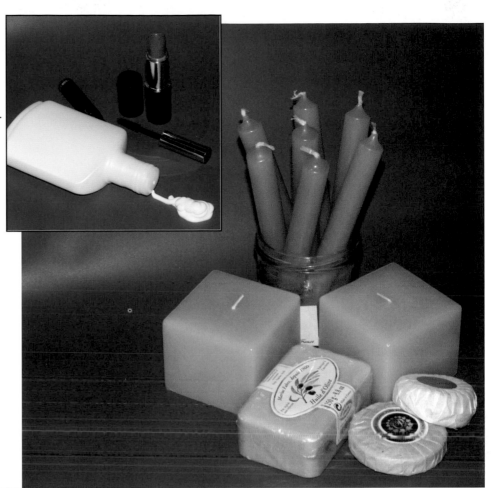

Vegetable oils and fats

• Most vegetable oils (like those made from sunflower seeds) are used as cooking and salad oil (left).

• Drying oils, such as linseed oil, are used in putty, paint, and varnish.

• Essential oils, like peppermint oil, add flavor to candy and cakes and are used in cosmetics, perfumes, and medicines.

• Vegetable oils are also used to make soaps, plastics, chocolates, printing ink, candles, lubricants, polishes, car brake fluid, and modeling clay.

OILS FOR ENERGY

Oils and gases release energy when they burn. We mostly use mineral oil and natural gas to heat our homes and to operate machines and vehicles. But scientists are now finding ways to produce alternative fuels (or "biofuels") made from vegetable and animal oils.

Using biofuels to heat our homes and run our vehicles would help to save natural resources, reduce waste heat and polluting exhaust emissions, and to prolong the life of engines. But at the moment, biofuels are expensive to produce. Soybean oil and rapeseed oil are currently the only cheap sources of biofuel.

Some power plants burn petroleum to generate electricity that can be safely transported.

Rapeseed oil is becoming a popular alternative to petroleum-based fuels.

Animal fat and manure, like that from chickens, can be used to make fuel.

THE ENVIRONMENT

Oils are extremely useful for our daily activities. We rely on oils for heating, cooking, vehicle fuel, and industrial processes. But extracting, refining, and using oils has a damaging effect on the environment in which we live. We are also in danger of running out of easily accessible mineral oils if our industries continue to consume large quantities of petroleum. If we are not careful, oils will soon become rare and very expensive.

◀ Wildlife

When mineral oils are extracted from the seabed, they need to be transported to their final destination. This carries a high risk of oil leaking into the environment and damaging wildlife. In extreme cases, oil spills can kill large quantities of birds and marine mammals in the area.

▶ Pollution

Drilling for mineral oils scars the natural landscape. The construction of roads and pipelines disturbs the natural habitat and wildlife in the area. Drilling also brings the risk of excess waste, scrap metal, and drilling sites that contain (and often leak) acids, solvents, and diesel fuel.

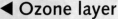

◀ Ozone layer

Over the last 150 years the burning of fossil fuels, like oil, has resulted in more than a 25 percent increase in the amount of carbon dioxide in our atmosphere. Carbon dioxide is one of the major causes of global warming, because the gas traps heat in the lower layers of the atmosphere. Other polluting chemicals damage the ozone layer—the earth's only protection from the sun's harmful ultraviolet rays.

▶ Alternative sources

Scientists are investigating alternative fuels made from vegetable and animal oils. Most diesel engines can be converted to use "biofuels," but at the moment they are very expensive. Liquid fuels, such as ethanol, can also be made from wood.

◀ What you can do

We have become heavily reliant on oils for our daily living, but our source of mineral oil is running dangerously low. If we all reduce our use of petroleum, we can help to conserve this valuable resource and help reduce atmospheric pollution. The coming years will see further developments in alternative fuels, made from vegetable and animal sources. Try and use them if you can!

ANIMAL AND VEGETABLE OILS

• Animal and vegetable oils have been used throughout history. Over 4,000 years ago, medical records listed "tree oil" as a natural remedy used by the doctor-priests of Mesopotamia (now Iraq).

• Hollow stones were used as oil lamps in caves more than 15,000 years ago in France.

• Rapeseed oil was used in the lamp oil industry, until the 1860s, when petroleum was refined for use in lamps.

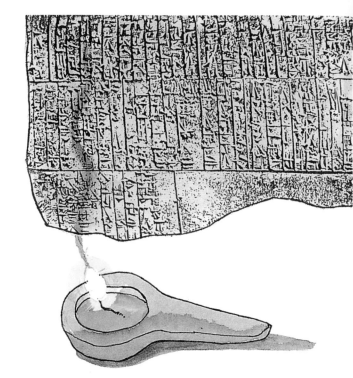

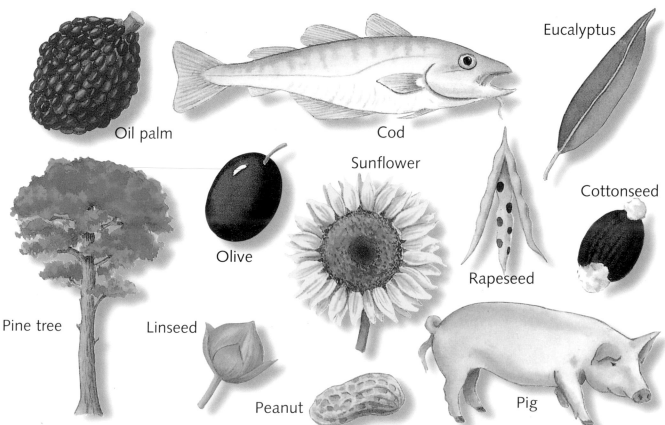

Eucalyptus

Oil palm

Cod

Sunflower

Cottonseed

Olive

Rapeseed

Pine tree

Linseed

Peanut

Pig

This diagram shows some of the plants and animals that provide us with oils.

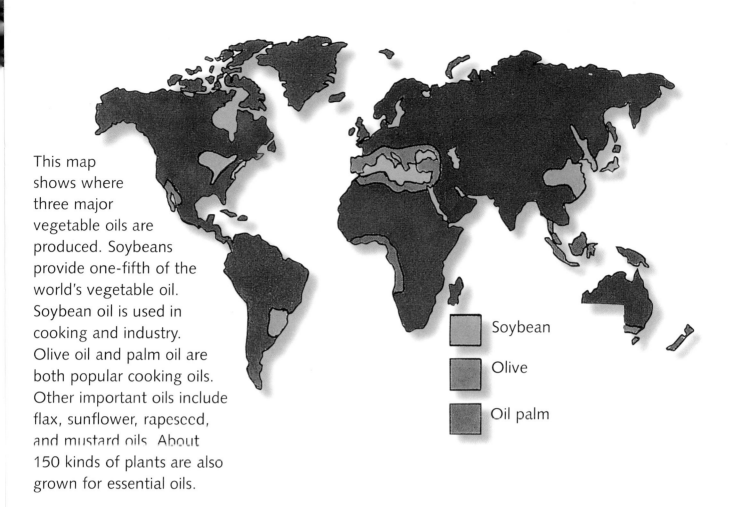

This map shows where three major vegetable oils are produced. Soybeans provide one-fifth of the world's vegetable oil. Soybean oil is used in cooking and industry. Olive oil and palm oil are both popular cooking oils. Other important oils include flax, sunflower, rapeseed, and mustard oils. About 150 kinds of plants are also grown for essential oils.

Soybean

Olive

Oil palm

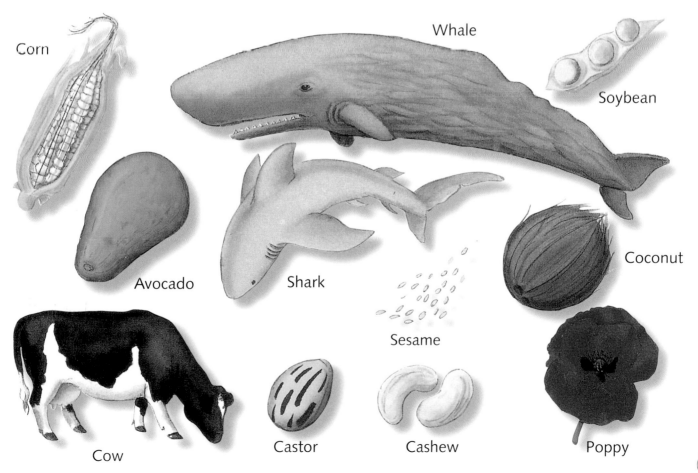

Corn

Whale

Soybean

Avocado

Shark

Coconut

Sesame

Cow

Castor

Cashew

Poppy

INDEX